SIOBHÁN CAMPBELL was bo divides her time between Ir lives with her family. Her wo journals, including *Cyphers*, ... *Review* (USA), *FM Magazine*, *Quarry* (Canada), *Orbis* (UK), *Verse* (USA) and *Poetry Ireland Review*. She is anthologised in the major contemporary collections of Irish poetry, including *Ireland's Women: Writings Past and Present* (W.W. Norton, 1994) and *The Field Day Anthology of Irish Writing*, vol. V (forthcoming). A director of Wolfhound Press, Dublin, she returned to University College Dublin in the 1990s to take a Master of Arts degree in Anglo-Irish literature. She was awarded an Arts Council bursary in creative writing in 1996. While living in the US, she has performed her work as part of the Guinness Fleadh, at Hidden Truths – the Bloody Sunday exhibition, and at the San Francisco Book Festival. *The Cold that Burns* is a second collection and follows *The Permanent Wave* (1996), a book noted for both 'clear-eyed compassion and sharp irony'.

To Patricia
and her aunty Bea
in memoriam –
with very best wishes,
Siobhán 5/10/2000

the cold that burns

---

siobhán campbell

THE
BLACKSTAFF
PRESS

BELFAST

ACKNOWLEDGEMENTS

Thanks are due to the editors of the following in which some of these poems, or versions of them, have appeared: *Book for Leopardi at the Year's Turning*, edited by Marco Sonzogni, Dedalus Press, 1998; *Irish Herald* (San Francisco); *Kestrel: Journal of Literature and Art in the New World* (special Irish issue), spring 2000; *Poetry Ireland Review; Stinging Fly; The White Page/An Bhileog Bhán: Twentieth-Century Irish Women Poets,* edited by Joan McBreen, Salmon Publishing, 1999; *Women's Studies: An Interdisciplinary Journal,* vol. 29, no. 4, 2000; *Verse* (women Irish poets issue), vol. 16, no. 2, 1999.

The author thanks The Arts Council/An Chomhairle Ealaíon for a bursary in creative writing which enabled the completion of this book.

First published in 2000 by
The Blackstaff Press Limited
Blackstaff House, Wildflower Way, Apollo Road
Belfast BT12 6TA, Northern Ireland
with the assistance of
The Arts Council of Northern Ireland

Printed in Ireland by ColourBooks Limited

A CIP catalogue record for this book
is available from the British Library

ISBN 0-85640-675-9

www.blackstaffpress.com

for John Doyle
who compares this work to
liquid nitrogen –
the cold that burns

CONTENTS

I

II

I

I sometimes hold it half a sin
To put in words the grief I feel;
For words, like Nature, half reveal
And half conceal the Soul within.

Alfred, Lord Tennyson, *In memoriam*

LYRIC

What could a lyric do –
get up and dance
to a tune of its own making?

And what might it disallow –
the lie in what is
finished to be fine?

And if, while it is dancing,
the hand in whose summons it exists
were to slowly wave dismissal –

no longer required,
no longer appropriate,
no longer the voice of the inner muse,

might it not dance on, oblivious,
moving to a music so familiar
we believe we have heard it in our soul?

NATIONAL GALLERY, OTTAWA

The room where sacred objects
are displayed is bright with hopes
that need not fight, now that they're
captured, catalogued and named.

Thurible, Aspersorium, Censer.
Who will tell they held the water
and the will, accoutrements to so asperse
those who wished the world less cursed?

The gallery plans an interactive chair
in which to hear the murmur of a prayer
and feel perhaps the warm breath
of believers on your ear.

Where reverence is called 'a bowing
from the waist', I know there is no place
for what I thought was real –
that words could fix their signal to
the heart and leave their seal.

That world is shrinking fast. We watch
the colour of our reaching disappear.

Will there be time to tell one story,
wild and lean, to curl the tongues
of even those who teach
that we can only fail to mean?

SWALLOWS

Sometimes it is possible to feel a memory
flush with meaning, to catch ourselves
as we stage a preservation.
Just now, it was yesterday's swallows,
spurting around the house in fitful sun.
I couldn't hear their chirrup but their flight
kept skimming the margins of my sight
as if their hungry flare-bred lives were happening
just on the edge of my horizon.

If I could search beyond that line,
might I find what makes me hold them dear
or where they garner their significance?
Perhaps, if something didn't interfere to sound
their song as though it were a happiness –
a joy that spurs my need to see them fly,
swooped out in their sudden arcs
riveting my inner eye.

THAT OTHER WALKING STICK

Her father too had an ash-black stick
he used to whack the heads off weeds.
He thwacked off the foxglove heads
with the stick he acquired when he was lamed.
He sent them flying, pinks and reds,
with a swish and flick of his black walking stick.
The pinks and reds flew through the air
like bullets sure-fired and purposely there.
The flowers broke apart the air
like gullets of blood smattering there.
With a swish and rick of the black ash stick
her father left the lane bare of heads
and the stalks remained alive though maimed
without their beauty pinks and reds.
Without their beauty pinks and reds
they lived on though seemed to be dead
while petals were scattered and smattered there
where the ashen stick laid everything bare.

PROGRESSION

Words draw meaning out of sound.
This is what my son is teaching me.
He says 'ih', points between sky and ground
And I'm not sure I'm seeing what he sees.

'Yes, there's a car,' I say, making a *vroom*.
'Ih, ih' is his reply while turning round
As if whatever he is watching zooms
And lifts up between sky and ground.

Suddenly I see the leaves are in the air
And on the ground and on the tree.
He knows this is his world, calls it 'ih'.
And he is right for there is thing and sound

And life. Soon he will learn 'tree', then 'leaf',
And say the world, word by word to itself.
Right now I can accept while he shows me
That we make up creation every day, and if

We say the verse it says, then sense emerges
Out of sound. But for how long will he know this?
How long before the ground he steadied shifts
And he looks up to see the heavens frown?

ORACLE

Whatever there was in the dregs of cold tea,
our grandaunt could say the sun would shine
for a trip to the sea, or how much to pay
for a dress. We were impressed.

When she took her age, moved in with her son
and her stories wandered far from form
(though they gathered truth at every turn)
it came as a shock.

She whispered aside her need to find
the china pot. She wanted to ask if his wife
had hit her or not. And the whole taste of
our childhood changed while she maintained

Make the tea and I'll know for sure.
Show me the pattern, I'll say for certain.

SAINT BRIGID'S WELL

I think myself a modern at Saint Brigid's well,
a believer that the people's reverence,
the ancient pagan way they hope
for goodness from water and a rock,
imbues their pieces of paper,
snitches of care-worn talisthings
with holiness, that in communion
with each other's pain they bless
this place and take their share of something
more than comfort, less than grace.

Why then, when a piece of sodden paper
latches to my shoe, its felt-tipped ardencies
askew, smudged and fading fast, do I
peel it off, will it to stay whole, find it
another niche within the wall, a finger-
darkened space, a den where yearning
can endure, and why, as I settle it there,
do I ask: if a prayer cannot be read,
is it any less a prayer?

SEVILLE CATHOLIC REVISITED

I PRESENCE

To these dark shuttered sacristies
the women come who do the churchly duties.
They bring fresh laundry for the saints
and sew new finery for Easter ceremonies.
They seem to sing beneath their reverence –
we of the congregation are the few
who may touch Jesus in his nakedness.

The statues fitted out with clothes
are strange to us, coming from where
any drapery is modelled in the stone.
Some are elaborate in lace and velvet
and have underthings. We think it means
this faith is close to flesh and bone.

And when we see that woman, working
in a side chapel on her own, as she leans over
and fastens His linen surplice like a mother,
we see her pain and its remittance
gathered in this loving gesture.

And we feel the sway of her quiet fervour,
watching as if we've never touched its source;
the only residue, a feeling that it might be rude
to guess her hallowed words.

II REVISITING

We think we recognise the stolid passion
of that small slow-moving woman
as she dresses the side altar on her own.
We watch as if we've put her there ourselves,
as if her honouring will mark the place
for everything we've lost.
But this is where we must take care.
While we can claim the incident
frame it as significant
lace it with a meaning that seems set to last,
we may find the moment lights only
our ever-hopeful eye, and afterwards corrodes
this wilful resurrection, this lie
that were it written
we would want to deem a poem.

TO THE POSITIVISTS

Is there a time
before we know of the gods
before anyone teaches us
before we hear them sing?
Then is your chance to ask
the only question.

We're told that music
enters the womb,
the season's light shines in;
we learn to tell the story of
our birth as though it is full.

In the juggle that becomes us
we capture any resonance we can,
craft these hard in our hearts,
though smooth because
they are so worn.

We looked to you to show
how reason finds design
but see you now in thrall to the world,
swaying this way and that
in its turn.

FAITH OF OUR FATHERS

How can it be that heaven no longer brims
from inside hymns?
The sound of that CD implies
that god is dead, long live the retrospective.
And at the concert (more a sales event)
that young choir in surplices is stranded,
left mouthing a melody that dies,
slips from beneath its own intent.

I took my folks to the concert of the dead.
'Thank you,' they said as we emerged,
although, like me, they felt rather askew,
until we heard a father speak to his grown son,
tell him there is nothing we can do,
that now there's only one thing left to lift us up
and out and give us back ourselves
and he was getting past that too.

REVELATION

I have visited too many churches –
the hidden gems, the must-see gold work
of a balcony, the stations carved from local elm.

They have become one great windowless
cathedral, holding nothing except perhaps
my memory of a toothless man,

hand excited under twill, who followed
my skimpy tee-shirt round the aisles,
raiding my insides with his bevelled eyes

until I left, finding the door at last, his rasping
breath pitched to a final sigh just as I went,
a sound that would thrum my drums for days.

It is strange to find his reach remains.
He took freely what seemed freely given,
stoked the fire of lust where most forbidden,

followed me to the side chapel, the special altar,
while I tried to shake the thought of his heat
ravelling the cool cloister.

You are not statue, he said, nor made
as virgin. You too have desire hidden
somewhere in your person.

Now at last I see he mirrored me.
She who stepped out into the air with such
relief was more myself because he

let me know we share
this mull of frailty and desire.
I feel my plan for him begin.

Could he now found the church
where I could touch another side of sin?

NUNSENSE

The nuns have had forever
to learn to score.

Assumpta was last out for
Eucharistic Congress in 'thirty-two.
Since then she sees the joke
in picking youngsters
for the TV station –
some special *Late Late Show*
about vocation. God, the excitement
they cause, and then to puncture
that elation. Or the time they told
Gertrude (only forty)
about being allowed a toiletry
for Christmas. She fancied herself
in 4711,

and her face when she checked it
with Superior –
now that was some kind of heaven.

HEAVEN

Habitually we believed that
Ever after was natural selection,
Avaricious cells reaching toward life:
Versatility first, the weak forgotten, and
Even in our tribes, we could see
Never – it's up close, written in our pores.

How then to believe in what is
Endless, strong enough to make an
Always to live by; a place where
Virtue deserves reward, though rarely
Evenly rendered, so we imagined
Nirvana, saw it with a swinging gate.

However, there always was an how-
Ever. No easy way to say for
All time and know it means that
Virtually everything is seeking,
Extracting, creating from
Nothing the last laugh, the
Lasting laugh, the yamming
Yes in the face of all our death.

NEUTRALITY AT EPERNAY

No mass will be said this day
of Our Lord. The priest reaps
a year's supply of altar red.

We work in the smell of boots
patched with tyre from cycles
that sheared the vineyard paths.

Mist at six
leaves the fat fruit wet
and darkening to our touch.

At first we worked too slow.
Now all we want is for the harvest
saved before it moulds.

We have become of one mind
with this work on this land
that has known death.

Our last night fête; the grandfather
passes round obscene cartoons.
We must feign laughter

for what seems like hours.
Clits and asses, horrible smiles,
captions we don't want to understand.

The night wears on.
We sober in the effort to maintain.
He, who has seen war, survived

to be so patronised,
now lets us feel our failures
have no charm.

STATUE

It stands in an unknown town in France
somewhere on the wrong road to La Rochelle.
It is blue, so blue
its shape at first is hard to see:
was it human or some monstrous face
out of a fear of our own working?
For the innocent victims of Bosnia.
It seems to have nothing to redeem it –
this ugliness that scatters the air around it.
Such bad sculpture
we wonder how it happened here.

But into the gape between
what it might have been
and what it was
there yawned a blue ill-feeling,
an ache that was absolutely right.

WINDOWS

'Once you set a bird free in the poem
they bring an energy all of their own.'
I took to heart what the poet said
but keep an aviary instead,

and watch a wren who tries and fails
to make a nest that withstands rain.
Her stick, too long, will break again,
she'll find another, also wrong.

I wonder what the shawoman meant,
how her bird would be different.
Might it hail from another world
not driven by need, a bird that knows?

But even my wren is sometimes bold,
she feeds in sun and fears the cold,
and from the way she tries and tries,
she must not know that she will die.

Feathers blow up outside the glass.
What is it they could signify –

her world so separate from ours
that she still sings, where we would cry?

As rain foretold by satellite arrives,
moves in, predictably, across the sky,
the wren and I stay busy busy busy,
acting as though what we make survives.

READING PHILIP LARKIN MAKES ME SAD

not that he goes too far, no, nor
makes things worse that are already bad,
but rather that his mourning is a whine,
a kind of god-free spawning of twentieth
century man, acutely aware of what
has happened, able to define, but not
prepared to build again a store,
even secretly, a granary to sustain
the winter, bring us through to spring,
some little myth to help us all grow old.
There's no help here. Only a slow tear
that burns the bitter cold.

FATHERLESS

Fatherless, we creep away
from all the claim
of that necessity,
our lives aflame
with possibility.

No discussion
of what is suitable
or of sin before it happens.
We are free agents,
irresistible, no overseer
now to raise our hackles.

What will we get up to,
who is there to surprise?
What measure on our actions,
immense in our own eyes?

We'd like a mirror to
our flushing faces,
some way to tell
that we are making impact,
leaving traces.

And when we talk
as if you are still there,
hear the pitch of our
own voice, remote and clear,

might we forget
we play the part
that held our lives to ransom
from the start?

STATION ISLAND

for Stella

On this island in Lough Derg,
crucible of altered states –
black tea, dry bread are served,
smelling salts to stay awake.

You took your body for a dip,
surprised the land, the shale.
Look at the sheened waters laugh
as your white arms flail.

He descends, hot breath in puffs,
cassock waving flaps.
'This is not a summer camp
for you who dare to lapse.'

I see you, red legs streaming cold,
pulled back then from the other world
but planning to reach for it again
come hell, come high, high water.

II

The world seldom changes,
but the wet foot dangles
until a bird arranges
two notes at right angles.

Elizabeth Bishop, 'Sunday, 4am'

WATCHING MY MOTHER SHAVING

Watching my mother shaving on the porch,
I wished I were those legs she tended
with her gliding Gillette blade, to feel
the care that drives her razor's edge, her
sureness as she works to leave them bare.

She knows these legs are good, imagines
their allure, aware of how they'll slip
from her silk sarong like a dare.
I want her to teach me all of this,
how to make things possible; how
to use my limbs to send a kiss.

But I of the flat chest and thunder thighs
must wait till she decides it's best.
Could that be now? She gathers her
gear into its special box. 'Never
never start to shave,' she says.
'That way you save yourself this trouble.'

I watch her walk her gleaming prize inside
then hug my knees so tight I feel
the inkling of my stubble.

NOTHING ABOUT DEATH IS WHAT I KNOW

except that it becomes a way of life.
You seem so near me I can smell your smell.
You could be standing, earnest to the last,
saying, 'We die, don't we, so let's live.'
Who are you now? And of your epigrams,
which have survived to be still useful there –
or are they what you leave behind to tell
us to practise while we can, practise until
we do it good, so good we miss rehearsal's end?
You did it well. But I still want to ask
if you knew that your 'let's live' meant let's die,
over and over to ourselves until we fade a little
more with every breath. Tell me, my father, are
you aware that what you left me is a way of death?

BALLROOM

My father's foxtrot could startle a room.
When he danced to 'Red Sails in the Sunset'
with my mom, you could be forgiven
for thinking they were matched in heaven.

But when he took me up to waltz,
I would be heavy on his widened arm.
I would stiffen the arc of his grace,
make the dance an exercise to learn.

He tried to describe how it should flow,
took it slow, replaced my arm;
but the rhythm that moved within my bones
would not be led where he would go.

In the end I was relieved to sit back down.
'Why so literal, Siobhán?'
I did not answer that at our convent school
I was being taught to be the man.

BODY

I watch my nails, white-flecked, moonless.
Here all the Campbell traits begin.
That flesh I carry but have never seen,
he knew it as his own –

when, to liven a bucolic scene,
a cousin closed the van door on my hand,
he carried me inside, afraid
his fainting child would lose her fingers

and while they were sewn on,
felt for the first time his own shrinkage,
remembered out of nowhere that nails
still grow, even while a body is interred.

Ever after, as he told the story, I would hear
again his surprise to find he cared.

INFLUENCE

If ever you looked in on me at night,
using the heart's door with some delight,
could you tell the reach of what you saw?
Flushed and marvellous of your flesh,
she who draws you through her breath,
for her you want to make the world anew?

The leaven of your look would show
what I'm afraid of but must know –
if in the presence of your sleeping child
you learned how truth can grow within a life.

For if you never looked inside, but passed
the door that would have opened wide, then
you have missed your chance to make a stay
and shame will stop you in your grave.

THE LESSON

To my surprise, for you I could not grieve.
You welcomed death as though it were your stage.
So many ways you planned to take your leave.

I longed to grant you a reprieve.
You did give love, in pieces, like a wage.
To my surprise, for you I could not grieve.

You said, as if proud to have achieved,
'I'll be long dead before you lose that rage.'
So many ways you planned to take your leave.

How could you think, much less believe,
That I, who looked on you as sage,
Would not be moved enough to grieve?

Your pronouncement left me feeling peeved.
I began to grow bitter, start to age,
While you prepared to take your final leave.

After your death, I admit, I felt relieved.
It's taken until now to work out on this page
How you planned to make me let you leave,
How you ensured, for you, I would not grieve

TEN-YEAR ANNIVERSARY

A thicket where I stumble;
branches to catch me
roots to fell me
birds to taunt me
flowers to haunt me
leaves that weal me
herbs to heal me
your presence to achieve me,
you who made me.
Do I come for you,
do you wait for me?
Can either one release?
I feel your heart
is urging mine to beat;
I sense your breath
within the pull of mine.
Is this what we may mean
by rest in peace?
The world continues
out of life and into death
and we are tiny pieces
of its rhyme that build
a new eternity in time.

FISHING

When we draw our dead near us,
reel them in, whisper to them
asking for their help,
and when we wish for them
what they never had in life,
is this not a prayer?
While its opposite rotates
as a spinner with a bait
and we wheel in the silence
of their non-reply.

THE FABULIST

She lived next door to us
in green suburbia, pebble-dashed
against the back side of urban
Dublin in those days that clear
the moment you think of them.
She ran her house like a ship.
She was the admiral, taking
the roll, calling all hands,
meting out inventive punishments:
you with the watering can,
for not making yours, you'll weed
that bed instead. When we visited
to eat her biscuits, she despaired
of us ever knowing the value of money.
She said she knew how many sheets
of toilet paper on a roll, her sons were
aware they could use only two.
On washing days she would sprinkle
her sails with holy water and a prayer
for drying. She prayed to Saint Jude
of difficult cases for her offspring
to keep trying. At night she sat
with a hot cocoa for the day's review.

She planned apple tarts, roast chicken,
stew; her cooking tasted as though
she cared. On her deck, you
dared to try for perfect fullness
Her stern look still cuts a swathe
through the general dullness.

SMOOTHIE

My sister is adamant she won't shave.
Even though I do not care to hear
the detail of how she lets it grow
under her oxter or elsewhere, she
takes time to insist she won't be bare.
'I know that women like plucked chickens
stalk the earth,' she says. 'I won't be
among them, I refuse.'

One year she said the time had come,
she was working in a bank, she would
conform. But when I sneaked a peek,
her tights still nubbed and bobbled
over growth; endearing – like a girl who
borrows nylons without telling her mum.

When we were together, this subject
would come up, as if I were an advocate
of creams or blades or wax. I listened,
aware of wildness in her eyes but
stayed uncomprehending, until the day
that she confessed; she was using
Chinese herbs for her moustache.

MARCH 3RD

Your life is coiled to spring into mine.
When you wake in the gurgled sap
you move on your own terms.
Whale fine, I watch you roll,
your back sometimes making a plateau.
You will turn my outside in,
make me live in a world you recognise
where the present is constantly becoming.

When I lay face down in a field to thwart
the will-o'-the-wisp that would take me away
in its whorled grip, was it your voice
I heard on the wind – 'stay down!'
With hay and dandelion in my face
I was calmed. You taught me then
but still I want to ask 'where are you from?'
though you may think I should know.

I wonder, before it's yet begun,
how long will our love time last?

Amy, born 5 March 1995

MILK

My baby's cry,
breasts swing heavy in their sling.
Milk moves in to satisfy.
My nipples have revealed their being,
red, sore and leaking.

If I were to call this what it is
would it disempower?

The let-down reflex:
oxytocin rushes in my blood,
fibres round the glands contract
forcing milk down all my ducts.

My baby sucks.
Milk meets her one demand
and more of mine.
Even that question must heed
milk's reply:
science of what happens here
enough to still all need.
My baby sleeps,
drunk on how her life fulfills.

FORMULA

The last breastfeed has been and gone.
I didn't know it was the last.
My breasts have shrunk so quickly
I'm surprised.
With thumb and finger I can squeeze
to feel the empty sac, no milk.

I would have liked more time
to wind away from being needed so.
But she finds rubber teats give even flow
and for less effort now, she's full.
Even here the engineered
makes comfort grow.

Tonight she may even sleep right through.
And yet, before I laid her down,
I held her to my chest
and hummed her sleepy song
for longer than I really needed to.

SIBLINGS

My sister would make the world
with her affection.
Her will unfolds its dark.
But her reach outstretches her
to disaffection
and her reason burns, a bellows
to itself.

Is she lost
or lost only to me?

I hear her call note
rail against the sky,
it follows the serration of her pain.
She asks how I can dare
to be this close –
and sends me to become
the one who's lost.

ST JOHN'S

To visit you there
became difficult, began to
stretch my care.
To have you say my name
and strip it bare of me,
as if we were in someone
else's company, someone you
never knew, nor who knew me.
It made us both so light
that we could disappear – you
almost did, gave us all a fright.
But then came back
to live again, though differently,
now always with that dread –
I see you keep it hid behind
your eyelids when you bend.
I see that it is dread of me
and of my kind.

THE HALTING

Love can stop though its stopping may be slow.
This time it is a shock, a real surprise.
Yet it is difficult to let you go.

What bound us is asunder now, although
Neither of us quite recognised –
Love can stop though its stopping may be slow.

I've felt the chill of my resentment grow,
Fed by past hopes and present pride,
Yet it is difficult to let you go.

I look at you and wonder if you know
that our journey's over, we've arrived.
Love stops but there's no whistle to blow,

Nothing to make a fitting finish, show
Us to be kind and just, not to have lied.
Yes, it is difficult to let you go.

How will I start, begin, to tell you so,
Or should I pretend nothing has died?
It is so difficult to let you go.
Love can stop though its stopping may be slow.

RECALL

Pitiless, disease and hunger spread.
Our people fled. We live now
knowing we are those
who bullied, stole and beat.
O'Hare, Kelly, Campbell, Helly –
take heed for we survived.
Our curse is that we've understood
what hurts: we know the will
that curls a feeding smile;
we have been merciless and thrived.

THE DO DROP INN

A rackety hotel on Galway Bay;
me, down from the smoke,
serving a summer in the bar.
I feel so at home here, I could stay.
Outside, a fiddler on the car port roof
practises tunes he will not play,
while those who want their ancestry confirmed
are eyeing up a man with cap and pipe
as if divining what they hope to find.

The fiddler tries a fancy modern reel and
though the wind steals every second note
I hear the inner curling of its pain,
the plaintive pity of its truth.
Just as I turn to leave, to cater those
we easily despise, I could have sworn
the fiddler stopped and lifted up his arm.
The sign he gave, that fingered V,
I've carried with me ever since, to warn.

WEST CORK

for Kevin

The morning is sodden,
the window fuzzed with condensation.
I've lifted the net curtain
so the light won't wake you.

Our last morning in this rented space,
a small white boxy
two-roomed excuse
for a holiday cottage.

It has served well as a resting place
where we returned to
after explorations,
where we warmed in a hot bath

after a swim.
Its bed has been good
for everything too, although
we must decide

whether to tell her
that wax stain on the spread

is a strange drip
from the bulb overhead.

And I am here eking the light
reading Boland and Mahon,
asking if I should regret
not having spent more of my week

on cerebral stuff – learning
the craft like I planned.
But I have to admit I am glad
that we drank wine together

and ate *moules marinières,*
that we walked the beaches
and saw a kestrel dive
from the upper reaches,

that we'll both take back
the touch and frill of fuchsias
and the breath of hedge
for soothe in the long
overstretched winter up ahead.

I'LL TELL YOU MY POEM ABOUT KILLING A PIG

I was sent home when they had it planned,
to get on the dinner, boil the ham
while they slit its throat, not a pig at all
but the fiesty ram. The squeal of him
in the kill shed. A burst of blood
over their heads. They came up the lane
when he was dead and always forgot I
was not there, the story never mine to tell
because I'm a girl and girls don't kill.

DOCTOR VERSE

This is how I will approach it,
like a man, clipped and sure
and partisan. Establish
the problem, identify the cause,
then possibly prescribe a ream
of love, of exile or of loss.

But what is a love poem now?
An affirmation within which
hope can grow, a faith we've
forgotten how to speak
that things, all manner of things,
can be well even though
we've shut the gate of hell?

Did we know when we gave up
being redeemed how it would feel
out here on the slopes where
literature is frozen in its tracks –
no beckoning heights, nothing below,
only an ice-laden sky and the careless
tumble of snow?

LEARNING TO READ MEDBH McGUCKIAN

I walked into your jewelled arumoured room
unclothed one day. Your cloak's tassels tickled
me pink before a sunken bath of asses' milk
and trailing petals – roses, of course. Floating
there, I felt the twitch of an expanding universe
in the nub of my nails that seem to root
my self. The stilled believing left me ready;
this time I think I can save it. In the act
of suspension I have felt the liquid and its edge,
seen dry land beyond that beckons, a fondling
about it now like home.

HOME AND AWAY

What is it that we do –
the lie we tell
the spell we cast
the mast we raise
and will it do
to keep at bay
the empty world,
the emptied world
where all is poured?

What is it that we crave
to make OK
to re-inure
to understand there
is no cure
and still believe
we make ourselves
at home enough?

The spell is cast
along a line
on which a bait
is primed and tied

then drawn back
to flick with skill,
on liquid surface
dances still.

We will still blame
the fisherman
though tide has turned
and managed stock
now swim the seas.
Could world begin
to look so strange
that what we crave
is to contain our
super selves
and rest within
the most fantastic
of our spells?

SON ET LUMIÈRE

Pointed wings, a yawning door, contend
this abbey's power though now so far
from any pilgrim's path. On benches set
between haystacks we view the
ancient order of royal France; each shift
of power will make the colours soar,
each battle lost will end in trembling sound.

Conscript and leper; heretic, devout,
time moves regardless of who's in,
who's out. Blacksmith and cooper,
fishing boys and milkmaid girls remain.
Their story lives within this acting troupe,
locals from the old demesne.
Just as I think what this may mean,

the bench begins to shake. We have a
giggler in our midst. It's you –
the very man I'm married to.
Can you not watch a pageantry unfold?
'Undramatic,' you complain; but look,

these players try their parts for size, they fit.
That cooper with his barrel, the women
chatting at the well. No need to act;

instead they make their history meet
their myth and in that, reach beyond this field
to everything connected and complete.
Within a tale of war and siege, the monk's
belief, the villager's adherence to a cause
is gripping, though I know they lose.

You claim no faith, but think of history
as progress that unfurls. The dancing
girls, the knights who miss their mark,
are all just that. I am surprised to feel
my sudden tears. Hormones
you would say, as we're with child,

and there belie my need to fathom
what our difference means. I take it
as my task, to trace what we have lost
and if we've gained. So that when
with our child we laugh and cry, we'll
know the import of them both, and why.

A GAME OF RINGS

In the padded warmth of a peat-black range
a kitten follows a fly, darts
between tin buckets full of water.
My aunt, who looks as though she's planted
there, slides a pot over the scalding ring
to warm up the dinner for her man.

My boots in the hall sound like a man
arriving in to sit by the range,
to catch results from the boxing ring,
and watch, from Sheffield, world-class darts.
I run outside to check the seeds I've planted,
drown them again with loving water.

I love when we go to collect the water.
Down at the pump, we need no man,
but swing the handle to the buckets planted,
carry them up to the sentried range.
My aunt has to sit when her shoulder darts.
She and I, the cat and the buckets make a ring.

From the pub, my uncle gives us a ring
to say not to heat up any water.
He's going to stay for a game of darts

and to settle a debt he owes a man.
We pull our chairs close to the range,
listen to wind through trees he planted

when they came here first, transplanted
from the south, from Ring.
They brought only the sturdy range.
Everything was different, even the water,
and she just learning to live with a man
who liked porter and sport, especially darts.

One time she thought she might take up darts,
knew at once he would think she had planted
the seed of wanting to be the man.
He could even have asked for his ring,
at the very least would have poured cold water
on her notion of living beyond her range.

But when her man is planted out of range,
she turns the frame above the holy water,
takes aim, despite the darts of pain, and throws a ring.